Praise for Leonard Temme's
The Rube Goldberg Variations

"Inspired by one of Bach's masterworks, Leonard Temme's *Rube Goldberg Variations* is a *tour de force*. . .To enjoy Temme's poetic imagination, one doesn't need to be the poetry craftsman he is; but in addition to the poem, having him reveal . . . how he masters the arcane rules of this venerable *ars reservata* is awe-inspiring. . . the work is beautiful. It deserves to be read often, just as the Goldberg must be heard often to reveal its intricacies. Both require a similar attentive interaction with the reader."

— **Frans von Rossum**

Amsterdam-based musicologist, Frans von Rossum has produced documentaries, programs on contemporary composers, and religious music and is the former Dean of the Herb Alpert School of Music at UCLA.

"In *The Rube Goldberg Variations*, Leonard Temme offers us a poetics of conversation, dialogue, and response. Reminiscent of Marianne Moore's seamless weaving of literature, visual art, pop culture, and the sciences, Temme's accomplished volume frames the poem as a space for bringing disparate things together. Within each piece, vastly different ways of seeing the world - and dramatically different conceptual frameworks for understanding lived experience - are made to coexist gracefully in the same rhetorical space. As philosophical as they are playful and joyous, these poems lend themselves to multiple careful and attentive readings. Temme is an exciting voice in contemporary poetry. Bravo!"

— **Kristina Marie Darling**

Poet, essayist, and critic, Kristina Marie Darling, authored more than twenty collections of poetry and hybrid prose, including Vow, Petrarchan, and Failure Lyric, forthcoming from BlazeVOX Books.

"The wonderful idiom, 'Build a better mousetrap, and the world will beat a path to your door' is often misattributed to Ralph Waldo Emerson. Regardless of what Emerson actually said, Rube Goldberg used the idea of the 'Better Mousetrap' to build his absurdist machines for newspaper comic pages. Rube Goldberg's exact opposite, arguably, would have to be Johann Sebastian Bach and his Goldberg Variations, BWV 988, which is a dynamic illustration of the musical variation form. The technically demanding music is named after the first performer of the work, Johann Gottlieb Goldberg. The playful dissimilarities between Johann Gottlieb and Rube delightfully perform and invent in Leonard Temme's *The Rube Goldberg Variations*. Using OuLiPo methods, Temme has created a sustained, sequential engagement utilizing the playful absurdities of a Rube Goldberg machine by using a few isolated words and phrases to create new poems with the vibrancy of a Bach concerto. As Temme reminds us, 'No one ever plans the regular.' I, as a reader, cannot help but admire this amazing collection. It is a marvel of a mash-up, I love the conceit, and the poetry fully matches what one would hope for! Hurray and congrats! It's a beautiful book."

— **Geoffrey Gatza**

An award-winning editor, publisher, and poet, Geoffrey Gatza, was named by The Huffington Post as one of the Top 200 Advocates for American Poetry. The driving force behind BlazeVOX, he is the author of the yearly Thanksgiving Menu-Poem Series, a book length poetic tribute for prominent poets, now in its thirteenth year.

"The interconnectivity and absurdity of the world is on full display in *The Rube Goldberg Variations*, a book of poetry that uses the inspiration of twelve-tone music, acrostic, and variations of double sestinas to create a sonorous, rhythmic collection that is greater than the sum of its parts. The verse ingests the writings of Heidegger, Hölderlin, and Heraclites before secreting these ideas back into the coda of the poetic forms. What begins as wordplay gains structural complexity in the way a symphony builds from notes to motifs. *The Rube Goldberg Variations* reminds us of how the universe unfolds from simple molecular building blocks, and that repetition and variation hold meaning for us to decipher in the mashup of natural, technological, and sociopolitical worlds."

— **Martin Ott**

Martin Ott is the author of ten books of poetry and fiction. His first two poetry collections won the De Novo and Sandeen Prizes. His work has appeared in more than 300 magazines and 20 anthologies.

"Some poets slice the world into jigsaws. Some poets traffic in arcana. Some poets polish gems. In *The Rube Goldberg Variations*, Leonard A. Temme accomplishes all of these. His are the manic gifts of the geometrist cursed with a mystic's heart. Haunted by Hölderlin, Heidegger, and Heraclites, this book reads like a hungry grimoire of irrepressible puns, philosophical glissandos, and stinging one-liners. This poet admits 'love will get you into trouble' but still convinces us to adore 'the madmen and the sandcastles they build.' These poems—nimble-minded, formally restless—deserve to be celebrated."

— **JOSH DAVIS**

Josh Davis, staff teaching poet of the Poetry Barn, holds MFAs in Creative Writing from Stonecoast, University of Southern Maine and from the University of Mississippi, and is finishing a Ph.D. at Ohio University. Recent poems have appeared in The Midwest Quarterly, Monster Verse, and Measure for Measure: An Anthology of Poetic Meters.

"Leonard Temme's *The Rube Goldberg Variations* is a book of poems that possess not just formal mastery but also a beautiful example to all of us how from a formal constraint a new understanding and precision can arise, and in this time, this moment in our country's history, when 'regular laws of logic are misleading,' when 'running in circles' we feel we are 'getting somewhere,' when we all of us seem 'trapped in the regular / going through of the historic tales we tell ourselves as burst balloons' - what a pleasure to sit down one evening and open a book of poems that goes to great depth to find clarity, that is unafraid of dancing with Hölderlin, with Heraclites, among others, to the music of its own devising. Bravo."

— **ILYA KAMINSKY**

Ilya Kaminsky, named by the BBC in 2019 as "one of the 12 artists that changed the world," author of Dancing in Odessa and of Deaf Republic, identified by The New York Times as the Notable Book for 2019.

THE

RUBE GOLDBERG

VARIATIONS

THE
RUBE GOLDBERG
VARIATIONS

Leonard A. Temme

Negative Capability
PRESS
MOBILE ALABAMA

The Rube Goldberg Variations

Edited by Sue Brannan Walker
Cover and Book Design by Jenni Krchak
Reproduction of Clavier Ubung bestehend in einer Aria mit verschiedenen
Verænderungen vors Clavicimbal mit 2 Manualen . Denen Liebhabern zur
Gemüths-Ergetzung verfertiget von Johann Sebastian Bach used with
permission from Bibliothèque nationale de France.

ISBN 978-1-7345902-3-4 (Hardcover)
ISBN 978-1-7345902-5-8 (Paperback)
Library of Congress Control Number: 2021939723

Negative Capability Press
150 Du Rhu Dr, #2202
Mobile, Alabama 36608
(251) 591-2922

www.negativecapabilitypress.org
facebook.com/negativecapabilitypress

An
OULIPO

Built upon a
Dodecaphonic Algorithm
of a
Double Sestina-Like Acrostic

Dear Peggy,

You awaken as my dawn. Sunrise
fills the house. With you, the colors appear.
At once they burst forth brightness to surprise
me with a wave of joy that you are near.

Here again with you, another day
begins my blessing, our good morning embrace
enfolding each other in the gracious way
that being with you being with me is grace –

– is our grace – a gift I live that fills
my moment-to-moment chasms, is the ground
supporting me, bathed in your light that stills
my raging chaos since our love is sound.

I hold you and behold you as you are,
clearly, a gift of joy, like Bethlehem's Star.

Love,
Leonard

*In the beginning was the Word
and the Word was with God
and the Word was God.*
– John 1:1

Contents

Preface   i

Introduction   iii

Section I: On Reading Heidegger

Variation 1:   Regular laws of grammar seed chaos   3

Variation 2:   Going rarely gets you where you want to be   4

Variation 3:   Occupations fill the time of day   5

Variation 4:   Best means going after one and only one thing   6

Variation 5:   Running any kind of ship kept the old windbag busy   7

Variation 6:   Love the madmen and the sandcastles they build   8

Variation 7:   Balloons contain your unspoken word; look up if you don't believe me   9

Variation 8:   Dusk, another place where we tremble in our running shoes   10

Variation 9:   Express stops at 34th Street – Herald Square tell you you've arrived   11

Variation 10: Under turtles madness turns to chaos, or maybe not, how can you tell   12

Section II: On Reading Heidegger Reading Hölderlin

Variation 11: Refusal, always obstinate, surprises. No one ever plans the regular.   15

Variation 12: We cannot help but start again; to set up in sharp relief the sudden going,   16

Variation 13: which does not mean it is appropriate to speak of occupations   17

VARIATION 14: Such paths in art and life distinguish content from form to
grope toward the domain of best   18

VARIATION 15: but not much light comes from such ever increasing
academic heat running   19

VARIATION 16: in keeping with anticipated dullness; or again,
as something lying present in *love*,   20

VARIATION 17: although technology allows expansion of self as illusion,
again like inflated balloons,   21

VARIATION 18: going through computations without life or spirit,
hollow automatons filling the dusk,   22

VARIATION 19: in a desert of thingness, blind, deaf and dumb,
but poetry is the acclamation to express   23

VARIATION 20: this most innocent of occupations rendered safe,
toothless by the illusions we struggle under   24

SECTION III: ON READING HEIDEGGER READING HÖLDERLIN READING HERACLITUS

VARIATION 21: Regular being, its understanding, in this context, transforms a going   27

VARIATION 22: Going where harmony is under siege, face to face with occupations,   28

VARIATION 23: Occupations do not beckon into being what until then is not;
nor is the best   29

VARIATION 24: Best is the plaint for the ever still absent holy ones, with its running   30

VARIATION 25: Running through these fragments is a want we might call love,   31

VARIATION 26: Love mounding from a nominalized death as absurd as balloons   32

VARIATION 27: Balloons, death's little nominalized inflations, slip through dawn past dusk,   33

VARIATION 28: Dusk, another time hack death normalizes to express   34

VARIATION 29: Express normalizations sprung of the hidden gods, releasing from under   35

VARIATION 30: Under its abiding power poetry as art can discover,
          recover and manifest the regular,   36

QUODELIBET: Regular old folk tunes   37

NOTES   41

ACKNOWLEDGMENTS   49

ABOUT THE AUTHOR   50

Preface

This book is a souvenir of many overlapping adventures, some spanning barely a day, others, a lifetime. One of these adventures was a childhood tour of the Roman catacombs. In my adult memory of the then child's experience of more than sixty years ago, my father and I are with a group of tourists passing within arm's length, skeletons and skulls lining the walls of a dimly lit cave, roughhewn through living rock. To see the large number of the remains of death reaching back over centuries was not at all frightening but certainly transformative. The vision was barbaric and primitive with no effort to soften or humanize it in any way. It was unabashedly itself.

This memory contrasts with the memory of our subsequent visit to Pompeii and to Herculaneum, which was a much different experience of death, that of a widespread cataclysm destroying civilization. In evidence all around these destroyed cities were the artifices of human activity, the sudden collapse of normal daily life with a sense of anguish and tragedy. None of this human suffering, so overwhelming in Pompeii and Herculaneum, was evident in the catacombs, which belonged totally to death. Maybe the cave nature of the catacombs, the experience of the underground, objectified death as a principle for me. Whatever the reason, this childhood experience of visiting the underground of centuries past provided me with a visual image of the unconscious.

I do not know where the catacombs lead. I do not know how they honeycomb the underground of Rome or the Vatican or St. Peter's. I do not know what one can find there of the absence of life, the absence of passion and desire; but the experience made clear the similarities between the human skeletal remains as indistinguishable from stone, mineral returning to mineral, calcium to calcium. Here, even Yorick becomes commonplace.

In that experience of the catacombs as a child, the light of my life, my consciousness, descended like Orpheus or Aeneas or Dante into the underground and saw the nothing of

Death, Hades, lit up by the momentary presence of my being. The profundity of the silence and darkness of the cave after we visitors had left, lingered in my imagination as an imponderable. It still does. All the world is a cave in the absence of consciousness. Consciousness lights the universe, which is created in verse three of Genesis; before that, in verses one and two, all is darkness.

Consciousness, of course, is a product of evolution, and I am not certain how much consciousness is possible without language or words or symbols. This is one of the deep questions of science, the embodiment of consciousness in other species, other nervous systems, or even in extraterrestrials. We do not know the answer to this, and may never be able to know because it may always be limited by the otherness of the other, which underlies what truth Turing's Test embodies as another form of uncertainty, limiting what is possible to know about the real.

What I do know is some of the power of language. We discover things as we name them. As a thing distinguishes itself from the background, it comes to consciousness and we name it. Then, once named, we can use the name to summon the thing back to consciousness. In our consciousness is its being. Scientific discovery is the process of discovering things that merit naming. This is the power of words to conjure reality, which is what Adam did, naming the creatures of Eden as God created them.

This book is another meditation on the power of words to create reality. It is also a souvenir of many trips through the catacombs that underlie or support my mind, enabling me to make discoveries and connections that I did not know beforehand; and once conscious, they shape the unconscious to which they return.

I am grateful to Dr. Sue Walker for seeing these writings as a worthwhile souvenir. I am still astonished that this book exists.

INTRODUCTION

The Poetry Daily email of October 20, 2019 included Gregory Stapp's whimsical poem, "Love via a Rube Goldberg Diagram," reprinted from *The Southern Review*. In a sense, the poem's title says it all, how love occurred through a series of loosely connected, arbitrary events. Stapp's poem equates happenstantial occurrences leading to an amorous moment in the real world to the absurd causalities Rube Goldberg diagrammed in the cartoon machines he invented, machines that fascinated me as a child with their silly, intricate cause and effect contingencies that made both sense and nonsense at the same time. I remember playing a board game, Mouse Trap, inspired by a Rube Goldberg machine designed to catch the hapless mouse. Now, much older, I marvel at the fact that so much of existence, at every level, seems to be a Rube Goldberg-like machine, making the sublime and the ridiculous indistinguishable. Inspired by Stapp's poem, it was a hemi-semi-demi quavering step to Bach's keyboard masterpiece, "The Goldberg Variations." A simple linguistic idea, the acrostic, connected "The Goldberg Variations" to *The Rube Goldberg Variations*, the one sublime, the other playful.

The acrostic is an ancient literary device that structures text so that the first letter of successive lines, when read in sequence, spell a word or a phrase. Although the technique is primarily used in poetry, the Old Testament contains a number of such acrostics. For *The Rube Goldberg Variations* I constructed a twelve-line acrostic with twelve words whose first letters spelled 'Rube Goldberg.' These words generating a twelve-line stanza, which, in turn, suggested an elaboration of the sestina, another traditional poetic form, like the sonnet, ballad, or villanelle. The roots of the sestina reach back to twelfth century France.

The typical sestina is based on six words, each the last word of a line in a six-line stanza. By following a specific pattern or algorithm, the six words generate six stanzas of six lines each. For example, if the end words of the six lines of the first stanza are identified as A, B, C, D, E, and F; then the second stanza is composed of lines with these same end words in the sequence F, A, E, B, D, C. The third stanza shuffles the second stanza sequence of end words in exactly the same way that the second stanza sequence shuffles the first stanza sequence. This repeated pattern of successive shuffling is continued to generate stanzas 4, 5, and 6 as illustrated in the table below.

	Stanza 1	Stanza 2	Stanza 3	Stanza 4	Stanza 5	Stanza 6
Line 1	A	F	C	E	D	B
Line 2	B	A	F	C	E	D
Line 3	C	E	D	B	A	F
Line 4	D	B	A	F	C	E
Line 5	E	D	B	A	F	C
Line 6	F	C	E	D	B	A

If a seventh stanza were constructed using the same shuffling pattern, the stanza would simply repeat the first stanza sequence. Instead, the seventh and final stanza, called the *envoi*, is usually two or three lines long, containing the six key words, two or three words per line. In this way, the first line of a two-line *envoi* would contain words A, B, and C while the second line would contain words D, E, and F.

In my situation, I had twelve acrostic key words that I used to begin rather than end the line; and I elaborated the sestina shuffling algorithm, or pattern, or puzzle-game procedure for twelve words. This elaboration produced ten sestina-like stanzas, each one twelve lines long; each stanza identified as a separate variation. The eleventh variation would repeat the order of the first variation. Rather than creating an *envoi* to avoid the repetition, I embraced it with the common musical technique of *da capo al fine*, which means that the piece returns to its beginning and exactly repeats it until the instruction *fine*, which ends the piece. In this fashion the first stanza is repeated in toto.

This is the structure of the first part of *The Rube Goldberg Variations*, and every time I have read this part, I am struck by the difference in effect between the first reading of the first stanza and the *da capo al fine* reading of it. The simple repetition of the identical text that begins the piece produces a powerful and unexpected sense of closure 120 lines later.

The twelve-word basis of the ten variations of Part I, with their formal, prescribed sequence of presentation, reminded me of twelve-tone music, developed by the "Second Viennese School" of Schoenberg, Webern and Berg, and the many subsequent composers they influenced. These techniques of musical composition are sometimes called dodecaphonic to emphasize the twelve-tone nature of the composition. I have long been drawn to the complexity and intricacy of this music.

At the time I completed the first ten variations, I was convalescing from major surgery and had time on my hands, which I used to read Heidegger, trying to understand the impact that poetry had on his ideas and writings, a topic he addressed several times over many years. I was reading his lectures on Hölderlin's "Germania" and "The Rhine," as well as a few of his shorter essays. The similarity of the principles of dodecaphonic musical composition mentioned above, along with the notes I made while reading Heidegger, suggested a way I might continue my game with the Rube Goldberg variations.

Since the first set of variations established the twelve-word acrostic of Rube Goldberg at the beginning of each line, a second set of variations might be possible with a double sestina-like structure using the twelve-word Rube Goldberg acrostic to end each line. This second set of variations also incorporates the notes I made while reading Heidegger.

The translation I read used an archaic English spelling *beyng* as an approximation to the old German *Seyn*, an archaic form of the German Sein, to characterize a primitive metaphysical aspect of being. Thus, *beyng* found its way into *The Rube Goldberg Variations*.

The second sequence of 10 variations ends with the traditional sestina *envoi*, but with a dozen end words, the *envoi* was expanded to four lines, each containing three end words presented in their original sequential order, 1 through 12.

The third set of variations, numbers 21 through 30, is a logical extension of the first and second sets, and posed a challenge I could not resist. While reading Heidegger's comments on Hölderlin, it became clear to me that both Hölderlin and Heidegger were in dialogue with Heraclitus. The three Hs braided in an almost mystical fashion, which I tried to capture in the third set of variations, with each variation warranting its own epigraph. Also important was the added challenge of combining the algorithms underlying the previous two sets of variations. Thus, each of the twelve repeated words begins each line in the appropriate sestina-like sequence, while simultaneously, each is presented as final words in the appropriate sestina-like sequence, but in reverse order. Consequently, the third set of variations consists of 10 stanzas, in which the acrostic Rube Goldberg words begin the lines in the standard sestina permutations top-down while the same words end the lines in the same permutation order, bottom up.

This third set of variations does not conclude with the typical sestina-like *envoi*, but does conclude with a *quodlibet,* as does Bach's "Goldberg Variations." *Quodlibet* is Latin for 'what pleases you,' and musically, it is a Medieval, Renaissance, Baroque technique that usually referenced popular or folk tunes. Musical scholarship has traced Bach's closing "Quodlibet" to a pair of old German folk tunes whose surviving text appears in the two epigraphs. The "Quodlibet" closing the thirty variations of Bach's "Goldberg Variations" is in a musical idiom conspicuously different from the other variations; thus, the "Quodlibet" closing *The Rube Goldberg Variations* is also in a conspicuously different idiom from the rest of the composition.

I hope it is clear that this extended set of poems, organized into three sections of 10 stanzas each, and patterned after Bach's masterwork, started out as little more than a verbal game, but grew into an increasingly complex structure. Whether the work is successful or not, it satisfied my sense of discovery in terms of the formalism underlying its linguistic structures, as well as my deepening engagement with the thought of Heidegger, Hölderlin, and Heraclitus. All of this is quite aside from any possible aesthetic value the 30 variations may have as poems, if any.

A word about OuLiPo may be useful. OuLiPo is an acronym for *Ouvroir de Littérature Potentielle*, which can be translated literally as 'workshop of potential literature.' OuLiPo originally referred to a loosely organized group of primarily French writers, mathematicians, scientists and other intellectuals interested in examining the influence on writing of various seemingly artificial, imposed, arbitrary limitations, regulations, procedures, algorithms, and so forth, exactly akin to the rules and regulations that govern the structure of the sestina.

It seems clear to me that all poems following a formal structure, whether sonnet, sestina, terza rima, or limerick, are OuLiPo but with a longer history than the more recent, OuLiPo-inspired creations. The imposition of constraints on creation, which is at the heart of OuLiPo, reminds me of a comment Stravinsky made in his 1939-1940 Norton Lectures on musical aesthetics. "The more constraints one imposes, the more one frees one's self. And the arbitrariness of the constraint serves only to obtain precision of execution."

That *The Rube Goldberg Variations* began as a game that elaborated into complex and thoughtful structures seems an important lesson about the universal seriousness of Rube Goldberg silliness. The being of *Beyng* seems to have elaborated into complex structures with few, if any convincing arguments for a guiding teleology. From subatomic relations, through our constituent biochemical machines, to our socio and geopolitical structures, a Rube Goldberg elaboration of logic through absurdity does seem to be the rule. However, the Good Prophet Rube added the essential element of delight to the whole process that can thrill us when we look closely at what seems to be going on. I hope you find delight in these variations as well.

MUSICAL NOTE

The musical score reproduced in this book is a facsimile of Bach's handwriting. The score was discovered in 1974 in the back of Bach's own copy of the published edition of the "Goldberg Variations" that he had kept for his own use. He made numerous marks, annotations, comments, tempo specifications, corrections and so forth in his own printed copy of the musical score. This copy, a so-called *Handexemplar*, is extraordinarily important, because it reflects Bach's thinking about the music after he published it, and provides clues about his own performance of the work. More astonishing, the facsimile reproduced here is from the inside back cover, and is a completely separate musical composition titled, 'Diverse canons on the first eight notes of the ground of the preceding aria by J. S. Bach.' This work, composed probably around 1747, was unknown prior to 1974. The back cover, a single sheet of paper, contains fourteen 'puzzle canons,' so-called because they require a great deal of musicianship to interpret. Properly realized, these cannons unfold into an extensive musical composition and seem to suggest that Bach had in mind a second set of Goldberg Variations. That there are fourteen 'puzzle canons' seems noteworthy, because the number fourteen, in one way or another, appears often in Bach's work since the number refers to his name:

B (2) + A (1) + C (3) + H (8) = BACH (14)

The Rube Goldberg Variations

Section I

On Reading Heidegger

Power over words is
power over things
— Milan Děžinský

VARIATION 1

REGULAR laws of grammar seed chaos

UNDER no circumstances confuse what you believe with what is real

BEST kept secrets spill their guts when your back is turned

EXPRESS what hides behind your words

GEOGRAPHY makes facts of fictions

OCCUPATIONS fill the time with distractions

LOVE slips out too easily; we won't use that word here again

DUSK makes every departure special

BALLOONS, filled with air, twist into animals

EXPLOSIONS have a way of cutting to the quick

RUNNING from place to place is a great way to make a living

GOING after one thing means going alone

Fine

Variation 2

Going rarely gets you where you want to be
Regular laws of logic are misleading
Running water has no feet
Under the sky also cuts to the quick [1]
Explosions never work the way you think
Best is another word that makes for cringing
Balloons, without air, remain troublesome
Express trains of thought on local tracks
Dusk rounds the day with goodbyes
Geography builds cartoons of real locations
Love will get you into trouble with an eyelash bat
Occupations don't amount to a hill of beans

Variation 3

Occupations fill the time of day

Going after hours is a waste of time

Love keeps returning no matter what we say

Regular laws of logic amount to a hill of beans

Geography makes facts of fictions or vice versa

Running shoes need their feet

Dusk rounds the day with a kiss

Under the Tuscan moon, a special kind of departure, forever goodbye [2]

Express what you believe behind your back

Explosions are cringe-worthy

Balloons explode too, beware

Best isn't so bad

VARIATION 4

Best means going after one and only one thing
Occupations is what we do with our time when we build castles in the sand
Balloons explode all over the place, such little bags of wind, [3]
Going from place to place kept old man Ulysses busy [4]
Explosions are also a special kind of departure
Love returns to fill holes with illusions, one after another, hole after hole
Express relations run through love like water, or the other way around
Regular science sweeps fictions behind selected facts
Under the veil of darkness we hunt for a way out
Geography spells limits between hither and yon, back and forth, yes and yes
Dusk turns the world into shades of grey, scattering color to the sky
Running a tight ship can spell trouble in the long haul

Variation 5

Running any kind of ship kept the old windbag busy [5]

Best to leave sandcastles in the sand, they're hard to levitate

Dusk begins a world of dreams, the welcome land of madmen

Occupations keep the madmen too busy to notice

Geography in the night dreams of castles in Atlantis

Balloons fly you over the moon into the land you've never heard of

Under the veil of darkness eyelashes beat him to an inch of his life

Going over the moon took the poor man's breath away

Regular as a clock, they knew he was cuckoo

Explosions after explosions tell the history of the universe

Express yourself, no one else will

Love turns laws of logic into a hill of pintos

Variation 6

Love the madmen and the sandcastles they build
Running in circles, she felt she was getting somewhere
Express lanes have longer lines, fewer stations
Best to just pass on
Explosions make the passing easy
Dusk makes what you see in the dark difficult
Regular as clockwork, she kept bailing, but not fast enough
Occupations do more than fill time; they explode busyness
Going never arrives, sad state of affairs
Geography, nevertheless, tells where going went
Under the blanket of work she hid herself with dignity
Balloons return well inflated

Variation 7

Balloons contain your unspoken word; look up if you don't believe me
Love again returns with its awkward silences
Under no circumstances prick the balloon with your silent barb
Running in loops she felt she finally expanded her world [6]
Geography told us otherwise
Express your concerns and desires, they amount to the same thing
Going home she felt she was making progress; he knew better
Best, she didn't bring up the subject like yesterday's potatoes [7]
Occupations filled their minds, instead of that dirty word, you know, *love*
Explosions follow close behind lighting the fuse
Regular laws of cause and effect hold only in a geography of balloons
Dusk rounds the universe with a kiss, that sweet end

VARIATION 8

Dusk, another place where we tremble in our running shoes

Balloons carry us back to where we belong, wherever that might be

Regular, I should not have run out of paper

Love, however does run out, like they turn off the current

Explosions make sense of time-zero

Under the sun used to cover just about everything, now it's parochial [8]

Occupations, such a long word for boredom

Running along doesn't make the goodbyes any easier

Best to have hidden it in plain sight, but isn't that what we're doing

Geography again, the earth quakes in its running shoes

Going returns since it ends the berg of gold

Express the strings of meaning you can never wrap your mouth around

VARIATION 9

Express stops at 34th Street – Herald Square tell you you've arrived [9]

Dusk never settles in under ground

Going after the big one means always living small

Balloons made of sticks and stones will break your bones

Geography of the heart and of the brain morph together

Regular as loss, wouldn't you say your mind is the world

Best to keep this secret, think of the consequences, like Elmer discovering himself

Love springs up like mountains in mist

Running over love is a way of dealing with it

Explosions birth the universe, again and again and again, like popping balloons

Occupations seem empty now, don't they, like popping balloons

Under all this verbiage are turtles, all the way down, like more popped balloons [10]

Variation 10

Under turtles madness turns to chaos, or maybe not, how can you tell [11]

Express yourself but consider your audience includes yourself

Occupations don't always work, but that's a four-letter word, as is word

Dusk comes before the *Gotterdammerung*

Explosions have their place; they're essential

Going up in flames smells a bit like the "Phoenix and Turtle," another "Liebestod" [12]

Running through all of this the tongue slips in its Liebestod, or is it the earth

Balloons popping, guns firing, explosions make their point

Love does sometimes seem to hold the whole shebang together,

or at least that's what the Schoolmen say [13]

Geography be damned, we're looking for a grounding, or let's pretend we are

Best to keep an open mind, let the wind whistle through

Running on empty, or nothing comes from nothing, nothings ever could

Da capo al fine

Rube Goldberg Variations

Section II

On Reading Heidegger

Reading

Hölderlin's Hymn

"Germania"

. . . and what are poets for

in a destitute time?

– F. Hölderlin

VARIATION 11

Refusal, always obstinate, surprises. No one ever plans the regular.
Consider the revival of classical antiquity. We're immediately under
the illusion that patterns have importance, implying that the best
somehow emerges, or the merely mediocre might do more than express
the commonplace, constrained by a map whittled into a geography
no more real than the conventions bestowing values on occupations,
or impelling a human face scrawled across the laws we call *love,*
but if we do not know this, how can we bear the onslaught of dusk,
for shame befits mortals stretching due limits like overinflated balloons,
which does not mean it is proper to speak of gods as though explosions
were somehow wise, imparting a particular significance running
through the commonplace, to set up, in sharp relief, their sudden going.

Variation 12

We cannot help but start again; to set up in sharp relief the sudden going,
a reaching through hollow verbiage toward common speech as a regular
picture, a mundane scene built with rules of everyday grammar running
through the prosaic we all know too well as the foundation flowing under
the constant instability of quicksand, with moment by moment explosions,
rocking every point that anticipates the origin we presuppose the best
of all possible worlds; since, from the outset, each one balloons [14]
into a nowhere while assuming the shape of an assurance we express
to anyone of what is runs in the darkened dark close behind the dusk;
for these visions emerge as an outline projected across a geography
we're discovering and labelling an attunement between self and love
in this space we occupy for a time, however tentative, with our occupations

Variation 13

which does not mean it is appropriate to speak of occupations
in this fashion, rather to speak with words that impart a going
together, a compass hinting how to speak either of the gods or of love,
postponing the final words and phrases until the end, so the regular
patterns are set in such a way they unfold a shifting geography
of discovery in a resonance of telling that is not simply a running
through a repositioning of words and phrases; but a settling of dusk
which anticipates the choice of words determined from the onset, under
the burden of inner stresses, a balance of whole form, pressed to express
emerging tensions of oppositions with respect to lines holding explosions
out of particular, ontological events, as much of poems as of balloons
seeking a tentative, if uncertain, path to discover the domain of the best.

VARIATION 14

Such paths in art and life distinguish content from form to grope toward the domain of best
though even this hackneyed point of departure doesn't justify its own occupations,
meriting its own investigations, yet the content-form distinction fits anything, from balloons,
to poems, and the form here asserts itself as an elaborated double sestina, going
through Heidegger's analytic lectures on Hölderlin's "Germania," triggering explosions
between horrors and banal prosaic constructions, even calling up the embarrassment, *Love*;
to undermine expectations that this is "really no 'poem' at all" to express
the question 'the slickest line-hopping and melodic rhyming' of one of Goethe's regular
singsong poems, with a gesture toward the greater power that poetry struggles under,
some discovered image, a cherished trope poets use to decorate a linguistic geography,
provoking academic investigations of connections pregnant with images, like dusk
heralding the eagle and snake of Homer to keep the professional machinery running; [15]

18

Variation 15

but not much light comes from such ever-increasing academic heat running
through lines of text and their explication to consider what criteria serves best
poetry's power, or the discovery of minute details it unfolds past twilight's dusk;
yet we need not be surprised, since image tropes fit the range of poetic occupations
or worldviews, darlings of critics who use fateful conjunctions with geography
to express unmistakable final lines, cycling through chosen words, including balloons,
to build local pools of coherence, held in the midst of near disorder under
patterns that fit well the personality of the poem, able to cope with its going
on, managing to assert a range of meanings, pushing line to line in a regular
pattern, showing us how to be acquainted with the text, ready to unfold explosions
of poetic power, blocked by habitual, every day attitudes about what poems express
in empty hours, for instance, as a fleeting form of spiritual aid or passing love,

Variation 16

in keeping with anticipated dullness; or again, as something lying present in *love*,
dissecting and explaining what we see, while others occupy themselves with running
programs, for example, or civil codes, or guinea pigs; each time it is we who express
the attitude to poetry, disposing of it as we will, but its power is to be revealed as best
experienced so our being becomes the bearer, enduring these textural explosions
from a being to which we struggle to bring ourselves, or that envelops us like dusk
at day's end, if we are to encounter ourselves as worthy of enduring the regular
beneath the poem as more than flimsy, leftover trinkets or artifacts of hollow occupations,
something best left nowhere; but can it be that it is not poetry we see as going
nowhere, but that we no longer experience its transformation of self in a geography
where self is undervalued to the point of a technology, and our standing under
our being commodified as we see ourselves increasingly mirrored in things like balloons,

Variation 17

although technology allows expansion of self as illusion, again like inflated balloons,

a situation that demands thorough examination, especially if it turns out that love

or can we say, with the ancients, Being itself, springs from confronting a ground under

the under of ground of self from which springs a voice, poetry, that comes running

to give voice to both the beginning and end of world periods, expressing a geography

of culture, words from the heavens of childhood, to base an act of life, to express

the first child of the human, the divine placed before the self as beauty or truth, going

toward the gods as a self-gift, immolation, entwining human with gods, when the best

and first child of the divine is beauty; the second always the religious occupations

born of beauty and love as a ritualized safe distance from the gods whose explosions

spark self-filling in the otherwise stark nothing of a bare skeleton trapped in regular

grey sloshing through the drudge of unconsciousness, the nothing lingering after dusk,

VARIATION 18

going through computations without life or spirit, hollow automatons filling the dusk,

trees without crowns, absurdly empty; columns without capitals, absurdly empty; balloons

absurdly empty; with no poetry springing like Minerva from the head of a god filling regular [16]

moments with streams of thought, sense, conscious being, reflections of a divine birthing love,

as the human adoration of the numinous so the sun of beauty thrills into explosions

bursting the merely calculable, the if A then B contingences we struggle under

the only way toward a space for beauty, past the commodification of our occupations

that fill the time with more doing, like a cobbler tapping at his shoes, the running [17]

of clocks, Coppelia's empty mesh of machined teeth grinding limitless moments, at best [18]

absurdly empty, hollow sequential A-B contingences without the internal geography

hidden in the repeating everydayness of experience without impression, unwinding going

down toward entropy, cast blind, lame and deaf with no impressions left to express

Variation 19

in a desert of thingness, blind, deaf and dumb, but poetry is the acclamation to express
a pointing to more than merely internal reflections but wrestling gods in the dusk
inviting thunderbolts without protection, standing open naked to power going
through the recognition of mere being self, not rummaging in the psyche or balloons
but the risk of exposure to god's breath in clay, the beginning word, Being a geography,
not a telling, but an eruption of clues of what we are doing here with our regular
habits, like carapaces, shielding our soft parts from the shock of mere standing, best
described as the miracle of not falling into thingness, but a beckoning of what, *love*,
dare we *love* in some non-trite version of a poetry that sustains falling through to a running
foundation of language naming, naming, naming, in the midst of quotidian explosions
the carapace almost keeps away, shielding us from 'this most innocent of all occupations'
seen from an ordinary perspective as valley and mountains shift, exchanging places under

Variation 20

this most innocent of occupations rendered safe, toothless by the illusions we struggle under
a cultural social artifact, like any sport or industry, the cobbler and shoe that can express [19]
the starting and ending of poetry, so that poetry is another of the meritorious occupations
adding to culture, a Disney cartoon; but then what are we doing but dwelling in a dusk
sustaining from the ground up, not as some kind of cultural progression but as explosions
toward the amazing shock of being, an a-historical shock, the inside of an inside going
on with a self 'full of merit' as we dwell in the structures we create between the running
of our being and the faces of our gods who beckon not as discarded playthings, emptied balloons
left from the time of the divine ones we can call no longer or we no longer call love
but poetic striving is harmless and dangerous, ambivalent yes and no in a geography
that tears apart the head and heart so all saying is not saying though we dwell best
with human dimensions in a world made human. No one ever plans for the Regular.

Envoi

Here the regular remains a constant burden, dulling under the best circumstances;
yet these lines express a foreign geography that helps me question my occupations,
but do I want them harmless when love, dust, and even the absurd circus balloons
carry daggers writ as explosions, enduring writ as running, and being writ as going.

Rube Goldberg Variations

Section III

On Reading Heidegger

Reading Hölderlin

Reading Heraclitus

Variation 21

Not those, the blessed ones who once appeared
Divine images in the land of old.
— F. Hölderlin

Regular being, its understanding, in this context, transforms a going
Under of originary commencement, of an originary running,
Best described as old M. Eckhart's offspring whose explosions [20]
Express, at once, those near and far powers, like freed balloons,
Geography, and other primordia, interred with anguish in dusk,
Occupations, and other such commonplaces we neither hate nor love,
Love being synonymous with ephemera, with occupations,
Dusk, and dusk's embrace from the skies spanning all geography,
Balloons, and their shadows like swollen clouds, eager to express
Explosions, if little else, despite the breath spent on a hoped-for best,
Running as a machine, careening without guidance, a language under
Going these sieges of self-doubt born of daily battles with the regular

Variation 22

*Men do not know how
what is at variance agrees with itself.
It is an attunement of opposite tensions,
like that of the bow and the lyre.*
– Heraclitus

Going where harmony is under siege, face to face with occupations,

Regular as Böhme at his bench, hammering with counter-striving love [21]

Running in apposed directions, mapping across a superficial geography

Under the oblivious sun, language, unable to shackle the unseen dusk;

Explosions, as a deepened, moment-to-moment divergence, express

Best, or not at all, a concealed harmony, the continued stress of balloons,

Balloons, those absurd membranes, vacuous inside/out domains, which best

Express momentary containment, delicate equipoised outside in explosions

Dusk of those we may no longer call with the heart's plaint under

Geography with no plumb, compass or stasis but with frenetic running

Love as a cleaving power proper to being, not the leveling out of regular

Occupations (poor cobbler) but the battle hammering out the ongoing going.

Variation 23

Ever since the 'united three' – Herakles,
Dionysos, and Christ – have left the world,
the evening of the world's age has been
declining toward night.
– M. Heidegger

Occupations do not beckon into being what until then is not; nor is the best
Going forward in some direction, filling time as though time were balloons
Love inflates with expired breath, since, from these originary explosions
Regular answers cannot sustain the failure of formulaic language to express
Geography as anything but arbitrary; originary beyng, being the under, [22]
Running, running through gods' lightning flashes, scattering the rising dusk;
Dusk protecting us with our fragilities and shortsightedness running
Under what we call *good mental health*, questioning how can geography
Express the blackness of the swelling vacuum that beckons and fills these regular
Explosions to support life's momentary scattered sparks and fragments while love
Balloons inside vacuum's negative pressure's expansion's ongoing
Best as inflation's filling void of oblivious, blank, pedestrian occupations

Variation 24

These, indeed, I may call no longer; yet if . . .
the heart's love has plaint, what else does it want,
The holy mourning ones? Full of expectation . . .
— F. Hölderlin

Best is the plaint for the ever still absent holy ones, with its running
Occupations beyond the grasp of logic, with its settling at dusk,
Balloons turned to thought, forming *intimacy* as a geography
Going from soul to soul, thing to being, thought to unthinkable, under
Explosions marking concord/discord patterns of regular
Love, that funny misnomer for the originary failures to express
Express, an equivalent misnomer for originary failures of love
Regular in its frequency on tongues, where *intimacy* babbles explosions
Under the burden that spirit redeems spirit in a predetermined going;
Geography, as metaphor for the beyng of ground, as are the balloons
Dusk casts over the holy mourning ones, with their occupations
Running with a keening plaint after some yet to be born best.

Variation 25

*The bow is called life
but its work is death*
— Heraclitus

Running through these fragments is a want we might call love,
Best grasped as a dialectic burden, or that which does, as its opposite, express
Dusk bound toward the sky's darkening sun; for as with night's explosions,
Occupations ache for non-being, being, the still wild keening over the regular
Geography across an infinite expanse of a one-sided taking, for such going
Balloons into a single-sided aspect to be rejected as a failed going under,
Under the other rejected single-sided reflection of failures that also balloons
Going radically through all planar views of what we call the normal geography,
Regular in its blind passed-over patterns through negations of any occupations'
Explosions onto death, if that is what we wish to call what might this dusk
Express with such great strength of non-actuality as to hold fast to the best
Love shrinking from nominalized death while maintaining its inner running

Variation 26

*What is first present in all
gathers everything isolated together
into a single presence and mediates
to each thing its appearing.*
– M. Heidegger

Love mounding from a nominalized death as absurd as balloons
Running toward the intimate openness of the quotidian, yet under
Express need to stand in the open beyng to discover self as a geography
Best known as ground, intimacy's other characteristic, poetry's ongoing
Explosions of self, startling as presence and absence through occupations'
Dusk to dusk timelessness of opened being to the intimacy of the regular,
Regular forever the primary open timelessness spanning the dusk to dusk
Occupations of being with being's radiance, the equivalence of all explosions
Going into the destitute time, the default of god, the failed best
Geography as even grimmer, a needless use for the useless need to express
Under the inaccessible simple of the quotidian bound with the incessant, the running
Balloons as absurd as death and certainly less defined or nominalized than love

Variation 27

Much has man experienced.
Named many of the heavenly ones,
since we have been a conversation
and able to hear from one another.
– F. Hölderlin

Balloons, death's little nominalized inflations, slip through dawn past dusk,

Love as the missing element for unfolding of poetry's work, the regular

Under pinning of nature, which is prior to everything, even the poet's explosions

Running through the wilderness of unbounded openness, its dangerous occupations,

Geography, and the accruing presence of the beautiful good that can best

Express the unbalancing wherein all presence confronts all being, doing, and going,

Going itself a process of unbalancing, be it that of a god or man, to express

Best every virtue, the abiding presence of the unfolding fabric of geography,

Occupations, or the unseen as the commencement of god's lighting running

Explosions through explosions as timelessness, or the keening plaint under

Regular nature, a voice begotten prior to the blessed ancient ones as though in love

Dusk provides the absurd nominalizations for death and its inflated little balloons

Variation 28

God is day and night, winter and summer,
war and peace, surfeit and hunger;
but he takes various shapes, just as fire,
when it is mingled with spices, is named
according to the savor of each.
– Heraclitus

Dusk, another time hack death normalizes to express

Balloons as historic fictions as are we, bound to the on-going

Regular gods of many names, their cries permeating a geography

Love fails to touch, much less embrace with no gesture toward the best

Explosions from which being, primordial or otherwise, could be running

Under our halting conversations, bounded by current occupations,

Occupations among the pliant, emergent images sustained under

Running spans stretched from node to node over gaps that explosions

Best approximate as chaos, the natural processes of a darkening love,

Geography, or the collective needs born of gods trapped in the regular

Going through of the historic tales we tell of ourselves as burst balloons

Express the normalized time hacks that mark the drop toward dusk

Variation 29

*The holy keeps everything together
in the undamaged immediateness
of its 'firm law.' Separating everything,
spirit remains attached to everything completely
uniting everything through thinking.*
– M. Heidegger

Express normalizations sprung of the hidden gods, releasing from under
Dusk the impulses that enable the appearance of the invisible in human occupations,
Going forth, gaining primal footing, always first with poetry whose set of explosions
Balloons into the being of the word with the word for the word, such divine running
Geography, reveals the madness poetry mines, the instantaneous bursting love,
Regular in all its forms allowed to shine forth, preserved in the appearance of the best
Best being the heaven's open holy earth, itself disclosed as the shining forth of regular
Love, the open field of play where heaven and earth sustain a permanent geography
Running to preserve that which comes to presence in and of itself as the world balloons
Explosions to render assessable those impassible realms of beauty unfolding as going
Occupations that are timeless since no element is lost, everything preserved through dusk
Under the constraint that what unveils itself as being conjures a power to express.

Variation 30

Everyday but wonderfully, for the love of men
God has put on a garment.
And his face is concealed from the knowing
and covers the eyelids with art.
— F. Hölderlin

Under its abiding power poetry as art can discover, recover and manifest the regular,

Express the thingness of the named, recall mind into mind with words, the best

Occupations of the gods forming creation, another regenesis of a numinal geography,

Dusk-eclipsed Theogony's struggle to embody its bases for being in love,

Explosions of the divine lightning gods hurtle toward their own absurd balloons

Going across infinities, flickers in and out of beyng, their shadows running

Running as more games begin, sparking their ridiculous inside out of going,

Balloons bursting in lunatic whimsy, their careless, heedless games birthing further explosions

Love declares with its heaven, earth, man, and god quartette, undistracted by the dusk

Geography gathering the whole infinite relation of these four in their holy occupations

Best heard as reverberant harmony, none one-sided, each with the other, tuned to express

Regular being, the four together as indwelling poetry with the ground being under

Quodlibet

I have so long been away from you,
come closer, come closer
Cabbage and turnips have driven me away,
had my mother cooked meat, I'd have opted to stay
– Old German Folksongs

Regular old folk tunes;

    how their melodies cry

        for love, for loss, for

            daily coming and

                going

Under the simplest tunes

    old sly fox, Bach, with

        cabbages and turnips both,

           never, never stops

                running

Best enjoy cabbage and turnips,

    don't be proud, don't distain

        the pleasant nether

           world, with it's simple

                explosions

Express sorrow, loss,
    be human, discover how
        you've enthralled
            yourself chasing
                balloons

Geography becomes
    important when you
        leave home, a stranger
            on the forest road at
                dusk

Occupations,
    their rich aromas
        filling the house
            from the stove, like
                cabbages and turnips
                    cooking, can win or
                      lose your love's
                    love

Love, you have been
        away too long, come
                closer, closer; now, enjoy
                        these, our simple
                                occupations

Dusk works magic
        over half the world;
                cabbages and kings,
                        turnips with wings
                              fill our private
                                  geography

Balloons are dangerous
        toys, don't trust them
                they trick us; with
                        them, we discover
                              what we dare not
                                  express

Explosions tell me
    of indigestion, of mother's
        home cooked-meals, of those
            twin deceits, worst and
                    best

Running above the old folk
    tune's ground, [23] old Bach leads
        Heidegger, Hölderlin, Heraclitus
        a merry chase; his laughter
            magic, easy, light simple,
                behind, before, through,
                under

Going on a journey,
    that's how you say it,
        the hidden genius re-
            working the Passion [24]
                Hymn disguised in all as
                    regular

NOTES

1. Page 4, Line 4: 'under the sky'
See Paul Bowles travel novel *The Sheltering Sky*, which was adapted into a film of the same name. To be horrific, it need not be 'sheltering,' the mere sky may be bad enough.

2. Page 5, Line 8: 'Under the Tuscan moon'
References *Under the Tuscan Sun* by Frances Mayes, another travel novel adapted for film, a romantic comedy/drama, which is to say that the shadows the Tuscan moon casts reach toward *The Sheltering Sky.*

3. Page 6, Line 3: 'bags of wind'
In *The Odyssey* Book 10, Ulysses tells how King Aeolus, Warder of the Winds, hosted Ulysses and his men for a month. As a gift to help Ulysses on his journey home, King Aeolus:

> . . .*gave me a sack, the skin of a full-grown ox,*
> *binding inside the winds that howl from ever quarter,*
> *for Zeus had made that king the master of all the winds*
> *with power to calm them down or rouse them as he pleased.*
>
> *Homer:* The Odyssey
> *Robert Fagles Translation*
> *Penguin books 1996*

4. Page 6, Line 4: 'old man Ulysses busy'
Unfortunately, Ulysses fails and returns to King Aeolus, begging for help. King Aeolus answers:

> *'Away from my island – fast – most cursed man alive!'*
> *It's a crime to host a man or speed him on his way*
> *when the blessed deathless gods despise him so.'*
>
> *Homer:* The Odyssey
> *Robert Fagles Translation*

5.   Page 7, Line 1: 'windbag'
See footnotes 3 and 4; Ulysses was himself a windbag, a great teller of tales and a well-known, cunning liar, not to be trusted. So, the great Greek hero, Ulysses, was a liar.

6.   Page 9, Line 4: 'Running in loops'
The Mobius strip: Take a strip of paper, hold one end in each hand, give the paper a single twist then tape the two ends together. Both sides of the paper are now one continuous plane. An ant walking down the center of the paper strip would walk on both sides of the paper and return to its starting point without crossing an edge. Such an ant's world is infinite.

7.   Page 9, Line 8: 'yesterday's potatoes'
"You may be an undigested bit of beef, a blot of mustard, a crumb of cheese, a fragment of underdone potato. There's more of gravy than of grave about you, whatever you are!" Scrooge to Morley's Ghost, from Dickens' *Christmas Carol*.

8.   Page 10, Line 6: 'Under the sun'
See footnotes 1 and 2

9.   Page 11 Line 1 '34th Street – Herald Square'
The intersection of Broadway and 34th St. is called Harold Square because the offices of the newspaper, *The New York Harold* were there, where Macy's Department Store was across the street from Gimbels Department Store. *The New York Harold*, *The New York Tribune*, and Gimbels Department Store are no longer; you arrive at a place that exists only in name.

10.   Page 11, Line 12: 'Turtles all the way down'
I first ran into 'But its turtles all the way down' in Hawking's *A Brief History of Time* and thought the story so cleaver. A brief search on Wikipedia for 'turtles all the way down' is well worth while. The point of the phrase is to evoke the notion of infinite regression, and the infinite regression of turtles appears in Hindu mythology. Wikipedia quotes Justice Antonin Scalia in a footnote to his plurality opinion in *Rapanos v. United States* (June 19, 2006. Section VII, footnote 14 – via Cornell Law School Legal Information Institute's Supreme Court collection):

"In our favored version, an Eastern guru affirms that the earth is supported on the back of a tiger. When asked what supports the tiger, he says it stands upon an elephant; and when asked what supports the elephant he says it is a giant turtle. When asked, finally, what supports the giant turtle, he is briefly taken aback, but quickly replies "Ah, after that it is turtles all the way down.""

11.   Page 12, Line 1: 'Under turtles'
See note 1

12.   Page 12, Line 6: "Phoenix and Turtle"
See note 10; also refer to Shakespeare's "Phoenix and Turtle," frequently called "Let the bird of loudest lay," an obscure, possibly allegorical poem of perfected love in which the phoenix is female and the turtle is the turtle dove male image. The poem has so many possible meanings that:

> *Reason in itself confounded*
> *Saw divisions grow together;*
> *To themselves yet either neither,*
> *Simple were so well compounded.*

The poem ends with a *Threnos*, which is in a distinctly different stanza form from the rest of the poem, not unlike the Bach's "Quodlibet" or the one ending *The Rube Goldberg Variations*.

13.   Page 12, Line 10: 'Schoolmen'
Webster's New International Dictionary Second Edition (Unabridged) (1934) defines 'schoolman' as: "One versed in the niceties of academic disputation or of school divinity; esp. [*usually cap.*] a philosopher or divine of the schools of the Middle Ages; a Scholastic." Much of Scholasticism addressed Tertullian's (c. 155 – c. 240? AD) question: "What has Athens to do with Jerusalem?"

14.   Page 16, Line 7: 'Best of all possible worlds'
We are all indebted to both Gottfried (lit. God's peace or protection) Leibniz and Voltaire for this happy phrase.

15.   Page 18, Line 12: 'eagle and snake'
Picking apart, analyzing, and following the threads of images, tropes, literary devices symbolism, etc., such as the eagle and snake locked in combat (see Homer's Iliad Book 10, lines 200 – 204) or the "Phoenix and Turtle" (note 12) continue to support an immense industry that can spill over, often unrecognized, into popular culture.

16.   Page 22, Line 3: 'Minerva'
Minerva is the Roman name for the Greek goddess Athena, daughter of Zeus and Metis, 'who knows most of gods and mortal men' (Hesiod's *Theogeny* line 887). Athena is associated with wisdom and warfare and sprung fully grown and dressed for battle from Zeus's head, splitting it open, but only temporarily.

17.   Page 22, Line 8: 'cobbler'
The tapping of a cobbler at work is the ticking of time, each tap the echo of a grain of sand dropping from infinity to infinity or the ratcheting of gears in a clockwork universe. See note 21

18.   Page 22, Line 9: 'Coppelia'
Coppelia appears in several ballets based on a tale by E.T.A Hoffman (1776-1825) published around 1816 about a clockwork automaton, a beautiful, life-size doll. A similar doll and ballet shows up in the annual, *de rigueur* performances of "The Nutcracker," also a Hoffman story. The central theme is the indistinguishable difference between life and machine. *Frankenstein*, born (published) 1818, and Coppelia are siblings, embodying an idea whose time had come with the rise of machines and the Industrial Revolution. And don't forget Julien Offray de La Lettrie's prescient 1747 book, *L' Homme Machine*. To celebrate Christmas we take our families to see "The Nutcracker" and thrill as Drosselmeyer gives Clara her gift, a clockwork doll, the tip of a profound iceberg of a question. For good reason Drosselmeyer is often more ominous than avuncular.

19.   Page 24, Line 2: 'cobbler and shoe'
see notes 17 and 21

20.   Page 27, Line 3: 'M. Eckhart'
Meister Eckhart (1260-1328) German Dominican priest, theologian, philosopher, and mystic, without whom the thought of Luther, Kant, Nietzsche, Jung, Heidegger, etc., is hard to image.

21.   Page 28, Line 2: 'Böhme'
Jakob Böhme (24 April 1575 – 17 November 1624) an influential German philosopher, mystic, Lutheran theologian, visionary and master cobbler who was visited by mystical visions as he tapped, tapped, tapped. His many works were widely translated into English.

22.   Page 29, Line 5: 'beyng'
As mentioned in the Introduction, this is not a typo but a conscious choice of an archaic form of *being* to capture an archaic German form of *being* (*Seyn*) that Heidegger often used.

23.   Page 40, Line 2: 'ground'
The Goldberg Variations are not elaborations, embellishments, or manipulations of a melodic line, melody, or tune, which the superficial hearing of our modern ears might lead us to expect. Rather, the variations are all derived from the bass line, the repetition of an unchanging figured bass that determines the progression or sequence of harmonies throughout the thirty variations comprising the entire composition. The diversity we hear in the music is running above an unchanging foundation; an essentially hidden ground forms the basis of the grand spectacle that captures our attention.

24.   Page 40, Line 11: 'Passion'
Jesus' betrayal, trial, and death by crucifixion as recounted in the Gospels of John and Mathew are two of Bach's extant masterpieces. His settings of the Passion recounted in the Gospels of Luke and Mark are lost; however the setting of Mark's has been reconstructed to some extent. One of the more well-known melodies of these Passions is sung to the English, "Oh, Sacred Head Surrounded," in the original Germen of the Bach's St. Mathew Passion, "O

Haupt voll Blutt und Wunden." The melody was originally composed by Hans Leo Hassler (1564–1612) to an anonymous 16th century poem titled "Mein G'mut ist mir verwirret," which may be translated "My Mind's Confused Within Me," which Hassler created as a love song, a lament of man's unrequited love, a yearning that may be the hidden genius reworked in the Passion Hymn of our daily life.

Acknowledgments

I have a lifetime of people to acknowledge, all of whom remain with me in some way. The list is too long to include here, of course, and it keeps getting longer as more people enter my life and leave their mark. Sadly, a growing number have passed through.

My parents, grandparents, and other family members and friends who have passed through, still frequent my mind, as do my many teachers. The extraordinary Marie Ponsot is my most influential teacher. She taught as much by her example and wisdom as by her formidable technical mastery and knowledge. I want to include the gentle kindness of Walter Spara, an amazing man, an unsung saint of poetry. Dr. Sue Walker continues to have an immense influence on my writing and life. I am privileged to claim her as friend.

Dr. Tom Frumkes and Dr. Werner Noell opened for me the beauty, thrill, excitement, and deep satisfaction of science. After more than forty years as a professional scientist, science continues to thrill, fascinate, and enchant, largely due to their continued inspiration.

I am blessed with many friends, notably our monthly writing group, The Table Toppers: Holly Blosser, Jami Buck, Diane Garden, Saundra Grace, Bonnie Hoffman, Mary Murphy, Donna F. Orchard, Dr. Sue Brannan Walker, and Dr. Ron Walker. I want also to mention the West Florida Literary Federation, the brain child of dear Ron Cannon. After more than thirty-five years, it still is thriving and providing a local community for writers. Other life-long friends are my real wealth: Dr. Jack Brooking, Bill Ponsot, Lou and Dorothy Provenzano and their family, and of course, Irving & Delora Vincent and their family.

Yet, without my beloved Peggy, to whom this book is dedicated, and our family, all this would be little more than dust. These acknowledgments come with gratitude and love to each of you.

Leonard Temme studied music theory, harmony, composition and piano initially with his father, a choir master and composer, then with several private tutors before attending Queens College of the City University of New York and the Manhattan School of Music. He has an undergraduate degree in psychology, a masters in mathematics and a doctorate in neuro-psychology. After four years of National Institutes of Health post-doctoral training, he held research faculty appointments at SUNY Buffalo and at the University of Kansas School of Medicine in Kansas City. He studied writing extensively with Kristina Darling, Josh Davis, Marie Ponsot, David Ray, Walter Spara, and Sue Walker. In addition to his professional publications, his writing has appeared in Commonweal, The Emerald Coast Review, Negative Capability, ALALIT, Half Tones to Jubilee, The Panhandler, the Best American Poetry website and numerous small presses. He served as Poet Laureate of North West Florida between 1989 and 1992. He is the senior vision scientist in an applied research laboratory.

CPSIA information can be obtained
at www.ICGtesting.com
Printed in the USA
BVHW092126120821
614280BV00003B/155

9 781734 590234